HOT TOPICS

LEGALIZATION OF DRUGS

Mark Friedman

Heinemann
LIBRARY

Chicago, Illinois

www.heinemannraintree.com
Visit our website to find out more information about Heinemann-Raintree books.

To order:

☎ Phone 888-454-2279

🖳 Visit www.heinemannraintree.com to browse our catalog and order online.

©2012 Heinemann Library
an imprint of Capstone Global Library, LLC
Chicago, Illinois

Edited by Adam Miller, Andrew Farrow, and Jennifer Locke
Designed by Clare Webber and Steven Mead
Original illustrations © Capstone Global Library Ltd.
Picture research by Ruth Blair
Production by Eirian Griffiths
Originated by Capstone Global Library Ltd.
Printed and bound in China by Leo Paper Group Ltd.

16 15 14 13 12
11 10 9 8 7 6 5 4 3 2 1

Library of Congress Cataloging-in-Publication Data
Friedman, Mark D.
 The legalization of drugs / Mark D. Friedman.—1st ed.
     p. cm.—(Hot topics)
 Includes bibliographical references and index.
 ISBN 978-1-4329-4872-6 (hc)
 1. Drug legalization—United States. 2. Drugs of abuse—Law and legislation—United States—Criminal provisions. I. Title. II. Series.

 HV5825.F747 2012
  362.29'15610973—dc22
                              2010044761

Acknowledgments
The author and publishers are grateful to the following for permission to reproduce copyright material: Alamy pp. **12** bottom (© INTERFOTO), **14** right (Don Paulson), **14** left (SelectPhoto), **15** right (Janine Wiedel Photolibrary), **17** (Ian Miles-Flashpoint Pictures), **22** (Gary Calton), **23** (© Catchlight Visual Services), **33** (Yadid Levy), **42** (Lordprice Collection); Corbis pp. **10** (© Tomas Rodriguez), **12** top (© Martin Meyer), **25** (© REUTERS/Alejandro Bringas), **26** (© James Leynse), **31** (© John Spellman/Retna Ltd.), **39** (© Ted Soqui), **41** (© Underwood & Underwood), **49** (© Richard Wright); Getty Images pp. **5** (Leon Neal/AFP), **15** left (John Nordell/The Christian Science Monitor), **19** (JAVIER CASELLA/AFP), **29** (Taxi), **47** (ANDREW STUART/AFP); Shutterstock pp. **7** (© holbox), **9** (© Gregor Kervina).

Cover photograph of cannabis use reproduced with the permission of Science Photo Library (Ian Hooton).

We would like to thank Kristen Kowalkowski for her invaluable help in the preparation of this book.

Every effort has been made to contact copyright holders of any material reproduced in this book. Any omissions will be rectified in subsequent printings if notice is given to the publisher.

CONTENTS

Some words are printed in bold, **like this**. You can find out what they mean by looking in the glossary.

NEW LEGAL HIGHS

Giggle Ecstasy K2 Meow-Meow e-blast Genie Demon Spice

None of these words sound like they describe anything dangerous or deadly. They sound fun, exotic, and interesting. *Ecstasy* means a state of pleasure. K2 is the name of the second-highest mountain in the world, a destination for the most daring mountain climbers. A genie is a fictional character with magical powers to make wishes come true for humans.

As names for products, these are perfectly chosen words. They grab your attention, they sound cool, and they are exciting. They could be brand names for candy or video games, or roller coasters.

Yet each of these words, in fact, is the name of a drug. And each of these drugs started out as a legal substance that anyone could purchase. Eventually, they became illegal in different parts of the world. Governments realized that despite their innocent-sounding names, these products posed a health risk to people. So local and national governments banned the products, saying that a person caught selling or in possession of the product could go to prison.

This pattern has occurred for many generations: drugs that are seen as dangerous are made illegal. Today, after years of drug abuse and billions of dollars spent fighting drug use, many people say that certain drugs should be legalized. And some people even argue that *all* drugs should be legal.

K2 sweeps the world

More than once a year, it seems, the media carry a wave of news stories about a new **legal high**—a substance sold legally but having effects that are similar to illegal drugs. Beginning in 2008, the drug K2 caught the attention of the media and governments.

Some companies called it incense, which is actually a harmless substance that people burn to create soothing smells. Calling it incense was a lie, of course. It was a way for companies to get around the legal authorities in various countries. K2 is actually "**synthetic** marijuana." A synthetic drug is created in a lab or factory, as opposed to real **marijuana**, which comes from a plant found in nature. K2 is similar to marijuana because it looks like a dried herb. Some people use it thinking it will create a similar effect to marijuana, but the effect of the drug is far stronger than marijuana.

Spice is a drug that is similar to **cannabis**, or marijuana, but it can have stronger effects on users.

CASE STUDY

K2: Harmless Lab Experiment or Deadly Drug?

K2 was invented by a college student at Clemson University in South Carolina who was doing chemistry research. K2 contains chemicals called **cannabinoids** that a professor was developing to do research on marijuana. A cannabinoid is a substance that acts like THC, the substance in marijuana plants that gets people high. Those chemicals that were invented at Clemson for scientific research wound up as the key ingredient in entirely new, more powerful drugs. To make K2, cannabinoids are sprayed onto dried leafy plants. In this way, the product looks like **tobacco** or marijuana. To use the drug, people smoke it as a cigarette or in a pipe. The smoke is inhaled into the lungs, which carries the drug into the bloodstream.

In Europe, K2 is called spice. It has been sold under many different, cool-sounding brand names—Spice Silver, Spice Gold, and Spice Diamond. As K2 became popular, health officials started to take notice. Patients started coming into hospital emergency rooms with alarming symptoms: accelerated heart rate, high blood pressure, **hallucinations** (seeing things that are not real). As scientists studied spice and realized that it was a potentially dangerous drug, governments started banning it. By the end of 2009, Britain, Germany, France, and other European nations banned spice and other synthetic drugs.

Though K2 was invented in the U.S., it first gained its popularity in Europe. Eventually, spice caught on in North America under the name K2. It was sold in convenience stores, gas stations, and online. There were no age restrictions—anyone could purchase K2. A U.S. state representative from Missouri said, "It's like a tidal wave. It's almost an epidemic. We're seeing middle-school kids walking into stores and buying it." By mid-2010, eight U.S. states had banned the substance.

Did K2 kill this teenager?

David Rozga was an eighteen-year-old living in Iowa who had just graduated from high school. On June 6, 2010, he was smoking K2 with his friends. He did not react well to the drug. He started behaving strangely, panicking, "freaking out," according to his friends. He was acting paranoid—afraid of everyone and everything. His friends tried to calm him down, but he ran away from them and went home. At home, he shot himself and died.

Iowa banned K2 a month later, but questions remain about Rozga's suicide. Thousands of people have used K2 without having such serious reactions, so some people believe he had other mental issues and shouldn't have been using any drugs in the first place. Opponents of drugs like K2 say that such substances are too dangerous and unpredictable to allow out in the public.

K2 is smoked as a cigarette or in a pipe.

Synthetic drugs never stop

Even before a nation grapples with one synthetic drug, several more may be on the market. Some wind up in shops, but they are advertised as products such as plant food or pond cleaner to mask their real purposes.

Just as nations were passing bans on K2, a new drug was quickly gaining popularity—**mephedrone**, which was almost like a cousin of ecstasy. It produced many of the same effects in users. First produced in Israel in 2008, mephedrone spread through Europe quickly and became highly popular in the U. K. in 2010, where it was called "meow meow" or "bubble love." In Ireland, people called it "bath salts." By the end of 2010 the British government (as well as those in Sweden, Germany, and other countries) banned mephedrone.

Yet once mephedrone reached its peak of popularity and drew government attention, a similar drug called NRG-1 arrived on the scene. Governments started banning it in the second half of 2010. Officials recognize that there is no end in sight to the parade of synthetic drugs. Micah Riggs, a man in Kansas City, Missouri, who ran a shop that sold K2, said, "Once it goes illegal, I already have something to replace it with. There are hundreds of these synthetics."

Ecstasy

Don't think that this pattern is new. For many years, drugs have entered the culture as legal substances, but once scientific evidence is found that these substances are harmful, governments act to ban them. For instance, back in the 1980s, people started using the legal substance ecstasy. Some versions of it were called Adam, Eva, Love, or simply X and XTC (letters that pronounce the word ecstasy). The substance was not new. It was first created in 1912 by the drug company Merck and was used in medical testing beginning in the 1950s. Back then, it had the incredible scientific name *3,4-Methylenedioxymethamphetamine*, or **MDMA** for short.

MDMA doesn't sound too exciting, but ecstasy sure does. While some countries such as Britain had banned it in the 1970s, it was still a legal substance in the United States. It rapidly became the drug of choice among many young adults, who bought it from dealers on street corners or in nightclubs. People found they enjoyed the good feelings and intense friendliness it created. Some people called it the "love drug" because it made them feel love for everyone around them.

Drugs such as ecstasy often become popular among adults in nightclubs.

Then scientific studies and media reports revealed some of the dangers of the drug. Some people were becoming **addicted** to it. Some had bad physical reactions, such as dehydration, anxiety, fainting, and sweating. Certain effects lasted for weeks. Studies eventually showed that just one use of ecstasy could cause permanent brain damage. The U.S. government banned MDMA in 1985.

But banning drugs does not necessarily mean they vanish from society overnight. Ecstasy's popularity only increased into the 1990s, and it is still a popular drug today, even though it is illegal in most countries.

Why ban drugs?

The pattern is very familiar: Drugs enter the culture, and they are banned, yet many drugs remain popular among users despite being illegal. So why do governments ban drugs in the first place if so many people want to use them?

The answer to this question goes to some of the core issues for why we have governments. Every country has different ideas about these questions, but most societies agree that we have government to protect the health and well-being of a country's citizens. And drugs pose many threats to both individuals and society as a whole.

Habitually smoking any kind of substance can lead to very serious health issues. These include various lung diseases and cancers.

Health threats

Scientists and doctors determine that certain substances are harmful to individuals, and governments decide that individuals who use these substances can cause harm to society as a whole. One main threat to society is health. Drugs can cause either death or serious health problems. Drug use also can cause severe mental health problems.

Economic threats

When people become addicted to certain drugs such as **heroin** or **cocaine**, their lives can be destroyed. They lose their jobs, they spend all their money on drugs, they lose their homes and possessions. Families are torn apart when a mother or father becomes a drug **addict**, leaving other family members in financial crisis. The negative effect of drugs on the economy reaches much deeper than individual families. Treating patients who use drugs creates a massive strain on a nation's medical care system. The money spent on drug **treatment** could be put to use treating patients with other conditions.

Crime threats

Buying and selling drugs is an illegal business. Those who control the illegal drug trade often resort to violence to maintain their control. **Organized crime** and gangs have been at the center of the drug trade for years, and the huge profits they make from drugs fund their criminal activities. In recent years, **terrorist** groups in the Middle East have been linked to the drug trade as well.

DEBATE: IS IT OKAY TO SELL DRUGS, EVEN IF THEY'RE LEGAL?

Some cafes and shops and other everyday places of business have begun selling synthetic drugs. Typically, the shops sell these products while they are legal but then stop once the local government bans the substances.

Right or wrong?

Do you think it's right or wrong for a store to sell substances that are known to be drugs just because they are legal? Do storeowners have a responsibility to protect their customers from harmful substances?

DRUGS FOR PERFORMANCE, NOT PLEASURE

■ Marion Jones is one of many athletes shamed by positive PED tests. Jones won five medals at the 2000 Summer Olympic Games but later tested positive for PED use. She gave back all her medals and prize money, and also went to prison for financial fraud related to the drug scandal.

People don't always use illegal to drugs to get **high** or because they have developed an addiction. Some people take drugs to change their bodies and increase their ability to perform as athletes. **Anabolic steroids** are synthetic drugs that mimic the effects of **testosterone** and other substances. For years doctors have prescribed steroids to patients who have problems with their **metabolism** or who need to increase muscle mass and bone mass. But some athletes use steroids and other **performance-enhancing drugs (PEDs)** without a doctor's prescription. The athletes take the PEDs to increase their muscle mass, agility, eyesight, and speed. Other than the obvious increase in muscle mass that anyone can see, there is no evidence proving that PEDs actually increase performance in other ways.

Weightlifters started experimenting with steroids as early as the 1950s, and evidence shows that the government of East Germany forced its Olympic athletes to use steroids beginning in the early 1970s. The International Olympic Committee (IOC) banned performance-enhaning drugs in 1967. In 1976, athletes were first tested for drugs at the Olympics. That year three weightlifters won Olympic medals that were later taken away when they were proven to have used steroids. Perhaps the most shocking Olympics PED scandal occurred in 1988. Canadian Ben Johnson set a world record and defeated American Carl Lewis in the 100-meter race and was crowned fastest man on Earth. But a drug test later revealed he had used steroids, and his medal was taken away from him.

Throughout the 1990s and 2000s, scandals erupted in many sports, including international cycling, track and field, wrestling, gymnastics, American football, and baseball. Some of the biggest stars of American baseball were accused of taking PEDs, including Mark McGwire, Roger Clemens, and Alex Rodriguez. Even as he set an all-time home run record in 2007, Barry Bonds was under suspicion as a user. One of the world's greatest cyclists, Lance Armstrong, has denied using PEDs when he was winning multiple titles in the Tour de France.

The public has reacted with outrage—not only because using PEDs is cheating, but also because pro athletes' drug use has trickled down to college and high school athletes, who are using the drugs as well. Steroids can have dangerous side effects. Adults who misuse steroids put themselves at risk for issues such as heart disease, hypertension, the breakdown of bodily organs, and psychological issues such as aggressiveness, depression, violence, and **psychosis**. In addition to these issues, young people taking steroids are putting their still-developing bodies at risk, an even more dangerous situation.

THE DRUG LANDSCAPE

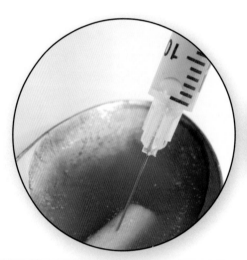
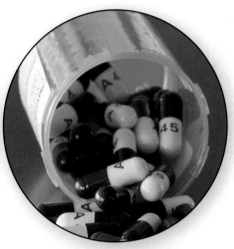

Category	Illicit drugs	Prescription drugs
What It Means	*Illicit* means "illegal"	can only be purchased with a doctor's permission
Legal Status	mostly illegal; some legal and regulated	legal and regulated
Substances	• cannabis (marijuana) • hashish (hash) • cocaine (coke) • crack cocaine • heroin • methamphetamine (meth) • MDMA (ecstasy) • LSD (acid) • PCP • ketamine • mushrooms	• opioids (Vicodin, codeine, morphine, Davon, Demerol, etc.) • depressants (tranquilizers, sedatives, sleep aids, Valium, Xanax, Ambien, etc.) • stimulants (amphetamines, Dexedrine, Ritalin, etc.)

Types of drugs

The synthetic drugs offering "legal highs" are not the only drugs that people use. People have used drugs, legally and illegally, for centuries. This chart is organized by categories to help you understand the different types of drugs and chemicals that are commonly abused and how they are related. Substances that are illegal are banned by law (selling, owning, or using them could lead to arrest). Substances that are regulated may be purchased, but local laws restrict who may purchase them or how much can be purchased, because of concerns about safety. Any medicines and chemicals should be used with caution and according to advice and safety warnings.

Over-the-counter drugs and retail foods	Household solvents
can be purchased in various stores without permission from a doctor	cleaning or repair products with harmful vapors that have potential for abuse; can be purchased in stores
all legal, some regulated	all legal, some regulated
• dextromethorphan (found in cough and cold medication) • diet pills • sleep aids (Tylenol PM) • motion sickness medicine (Dramamine) • energy drinks (Red Bull, etc.) • caffeine (coffee) • alcohol • tobacco	• adhesives (glue) • spray paint • lighter fluid • paint thinner • correction fluid (White-Out) • gasoline • nitrous oxide (whipped cream chargers) • amyl nitrites/"poppers" (air freshener)

CAN WE WIN THE WAR ON DRUGS?

One of the more unsettling facts about the drug scene today is that the many new, synthetic drugs arriving every year are only the tip of the iceberg. Other illicit drugs have been used for generations and are still common, such as marijuana, heroin, and cocaine. And widespread alcohol and tobacco continue to create health issues for millions of people. For decades, governments have been waging a "war on drugs"— the question is, how can this war be won?

In an actual war, military commanders must create strategies to fight on several "fronts"—locations where one army meets the opponent. In the war on drugs, there are several fronts, but none is a specific location. The war involves two main fronts:

- fighting supply (stopping people who grow, **manufacture**, and transport drugs)

- fighting demand (reducing the desire to buy and use drugs through laws, prevention, and education)

Where does the supply start?

You might think that the easiest way to stop people from using drugs is to simply stop the drug trade—the network of individuals and companies who make, transport, and sell drugs. But this network is more like a massive, sticky spider web.

A European law-enforcement officer finds cannabis plants during a drug raid.

WHO DECLARED WAR?

U.S. President Richard Nixon first used the term *war on drugs* in 1971. At the time, the United States was involved in the Vietnam War—a war that was hugely unpopular among a large segment of the U.S. population. The era was also marked by a massive increase in drug use among young people, beginning in the 1960s. American soldiers were returning from Vietnam addicted to heroin, which was available and inexpensive in Asian countries where they had been stationed. Nixon first talked about a war on drugs to address the problem of drug use in the military. But the U.S. and other governments also waged a war against drug use in all parts of society.

Reconstructive procedures

Locating drug manufacturers is the first issue. The ingredients for illicit drugs are made in many different countries. Some countries have the right climate or geography to grow a certain plant; in other cases, a national government allows or encourages the growth and manufacturing of drugs.

- Cocaine is derived from the coca plant, which is grown mostly in the Andes mountain region of South America. Colombia is the largest producer of coca, while Bolivia and Peru are also major producers.

- Heroin is made from the opium poppy plant. Afghanistan is by far the world's largest producer of opium poppies, with Burma, Colombia, and Mexico also major producers.

- Marijuana and **hashish** are made from the cannabis plant. Cannabis is relatively easy to grow, so it is produced just about everywhere. Mexico is the leading producer, but countries from Canada to Ghana to Nepal to Kazakhstan also produce large amounts.

- Synthetic drugs are made in labs or factories, so they do not rely on a climate or geography for growing. The Netherlands, Poland, and other Eastern European countries are major manufacturers. In recent years, China has been identified as a producer of new "legal high" products.

How do drugs travel?

Once drugs are manufactured, they must be transported. Large-scale drug growers or makers cannot simply ship their products to their customers as ordinary manufacturers do. So a vast network of "**traffickers**" participate in moving the product from one location to another. They often cross several international borders where they have to evade government agents. Eventually the drug arrives in the place where it will be sold to customers. Many countries of the world are not involved in making drugs, but they are key locations in trafficking. Like a street intersection, these countries are places where one person brings drugs in, and another person takes them to the next destination.

DEALING WITH FOREIGN GOVERNMENTS

The United States has been the major player in attempting to stop drug production and traffic. The U.S. government has used many tactics with many countries.

- *Military aid:* The United States sends millions of dollars every year to countries such as Colombia. Colombia is supposed to use that money to maintain a military to stop drug production and trafficking. But while Colombia has accepted this American aid, its government has also been accused of accepting money from **drug lords**.

- *Military force:* In 1989, the United States invaded Panama to stop its leader, Manuel Noriega, who was supporting drug traffickers. But some nations object to the United States using military force in this way. They say that the military should only be used in response to a military threat from another nation.

- *Crop killing:* U.S. planes regularly fly over foreign countries to spray poison on drug crops to kill the plants. But some growers harvest the crops anyway, and they allow poisoned drugs to enter the market.

Right or wrong?

Do you think it's right or wrong for one nation to exert its will on other nations in these ways, in order to stop the flow of drugs?

■ Police officials in Colombia inspect coca plants at a cocaine laboratory before destroying the site.

For instance, Costa Rica is a major traffic center for drugs traveling from South America to North America. Likewise, Greece is a gateway for traffickers taking drugs from Asia and the Middle East into European countries. Nigeria is one of the major drug-traffic centers in Africa. A country can become a drug-traffic hub (center) based on its geography (how close it is to other countries, or if it is a sea port) and how well its government controls drug trade.

Attacking demand

Supply and demand are two forces of an economy that work hand in hand. The "demand" is the amount of a product that the economy wants. Think about any product in your local supermarket. You can tell there is a tremendous demand for breakfast cereal because an entire aisle has dozens of cereal brands. All those cereal brands are in the store because consumers have shown they want them—there is a strong *demand* for cereal.

On the other hand, there is probably a very small area in your supermarket with canned sardines. Fewer people like sardines compared to cereal, so sardines have a much smaller demand.

Cereal and sardines, of course, have nothing to do with illicit drugs, except that the laws of supply and demand affect these products in much the same way. There is a tremendous demand for drugs by consumers—many people want to use drugs. Even though people have been educated about the risks of drug use, the demand for drugs continues. So if there is demand, somebody will figure out how to create a supply. Governments and physicians around the world have worked hard to decrease the demand for drugs.

Making drugs illegal

The most frequently used tool for stopping the demand for drugs is to pass laws that outlaw drugs. Governments intend for drug laws to serve two purposes: (1) punish those who use illegal drugs, and (2) discourage others from using drugs by making them fear the consequences. Drug laws vary from nation to nation.

The United Kingdom

In the United Kingdom, the Misuse of Drugs Act of 1971 created a three-step system for classifying drugs. Class A includes the most dangerous drugs, such as cocaine, MDMA, heroin, and **LSD**.

Class B includes less dangerous drugs (amphetamines, codeine, cannabis, etc.). Class C includes even less dangerous drugs (steroids, tranquilizers, etc.). The maximum penalties for drug convictions is most harsh for Class A drugs and less harsh for Class B and C drugs. For instance, if you are convicted of possessing a Class A drug, you could go to prison for seven years, but only five years for a Class B drug and two years for a Class C drug. Individual courts decide on exact sentences based on guidelines and the circumstances of individual cases.

United States

The United States has a similar system, but it has five categories. Australia has nine categories. No matter what the system is, nearly all nations have drug laws that place harsh penalties on possession of drugs and even harsher penalties on selling or distributing drugs. And the laws are put into practice. In the United States, over 1.6 million people are arrested for drug possession every year. That's about 12 percent of all arrests for all types of crime. Getting arrested for drug possession can ruin a person's reputation, education, and career in one swift motion.

Southeast Asia

Southeast Asian countries are known to have some of the strictest drug laws in the world. For instance, Singapore law says that if a person is simply caught in a room where drugs are being used, that person can be arrested for drug use. Even if a person has the keys to a building where drugs are found, the person can be arrested. Several countries (Singapore, Indonesia, Malaysia, and Vietnam) impose a death sentence on drug traffickers.

Middle Eastern countries

Many Middle Eastern countries with Arab governments have extremely strict drug laws. In the United Arab Emirates, a person who is caught with any tiny amount of drugs can be imprisoned for a minimum of four years. In one recent case, a Swiss traveler in Dubai was arrested and jailed for four years when three poppy seeds from a bread roll were found on his clothing. Poppies are the plant used to make heroin.

Treating users

Why do people use drugs? For some, they want to experiment with something new. Many take this risk once or twice and never use drugs again. Others form a habit that leads them to use drugs repeatedly. And for others, the habit grows into an addiction—a medical condition in which people cannot stop themselves from using a drug. Drug addiction can lead to serious health problems and even death.

There are many ways of treating drug addiction, and the treatment depends on the type of drug(s) involved. Most treatment involves behavioral therapy (seeking counseling alone or in a group, with a psychiatrist or social worker). Addiction to certain drugs also requires medical treatment. Heroin, for instance, creates a physical addiction— the body relies on the drug to function properly. To suddenly stop using heroin causes the body to react with terrible symptoms, including sweating, fever, and vomiting. So addicts are given different drugs, such as methadone, to help them through withdrawal (a period of time when the body is trained to function without the drug). For some patients who have a severe addiction, doctors actually prescribe daily heroin injections that patients receive in a clinic. The patients gradually reduce the doses until they break their addiction.

A police officer discovers drugs in the pockets of a criminal suspect. Governments devote countless police resources to tracking down and arresting drug dealers and users.

Government money

Governments spend money on treatment because they believe it saves more money in the long run. If a drug addict can be successfully treated, that person will avoid future arrests and imprisonment, which cost the government money. Also, a person who has been treated can go to work and be a productive member of society, further helping us all. A 2001 report by the U.S. Center for Substance Abuse Treatment found that every $1 spent on treatment would eventually save society $3 in the future.

Many health officials believe that more money should be devoted to counseling and medical treatment for drug users.

THE POWER OF WORDS: *THE WAR ON DRUGS*

Is the war on drugs really a war? The true definition of *war* is a struggle between opposing forces. Drugs are just chemicals and plants. They have no will, and they cannot act on their own. The real opponents in this war are the drug suppliers, who provide the drugs that destroy lives. But for the most part, drug suppliers are not nations, and governments usually go to war against nations.

Critics of drug laws say that by using the term *war on drugs*, governments create a false sense that their nation is in an actual war. And in war, governments should be given special powers. For instance, in wartime, citizens tend to willingly sacrifice certain privileges and individual liberties (freedoms) to assist the government in winning the war. They may also be willing to pay higher taxes to fund the war effort.

Think about the following statements. Decide whether you agree or disagree with each.

1. In times of war, police should be able to enter a home without a warrant and search for suspected war criminals.

2. In times of war, government agents should be able to intercept e-mail and listen to private phone conversations to track down war criminals.

3. In times of war, our military should be able to invade enemy countries to stop their war efforts.

Now, remove all references to "war" in these statements. The following statements only refer to drugs, and they describe a time when our country is *not* at war.

1. Police should be able to enter a home without a warrant and search for suspected drug users.

2. Government agents should be able to intercept e-mail and listen to private phone conversations to track down drug users.

3. The military should be able to invade other countries to stop their drug-production efforts.

Are your agree/disagree responses any different? Why or why not?

Soldiers stand on piles of drugs before the drugs were incinerated at a military base in Mexico. According to local media, soldiers burned more than 4,409 pounds (2,000 kilograms) of marijuana and cocaine along with other drugs seized during different military and police operations.

EDUCATION: THE BEST SOLUTION?

Since the 1980s, programs like DARE bring drug-abuse education directly to sudents in their schools.

Those who disagree about the effectiveness of drug laws do agree that education is the best long-term strategy for preventing people from becoming drug users. Education programs can be targeted at teenagers and children to teach the true risks of drug use before kids have the opportunity to experiment with drugs out of curiosity. These programs also aim to set young people up for a healthy, drug-free adult life.

One of the largest education programs is DARE (Drug Abuse Resistance Education). It was launched in 1983 in the United States and is now used in more than forty countries, including Canada, Britain, and Japan. The program is run by local police officers who come into classrooms and lecture, lead discussions, and show videos. As widespread as DARE is, it is just an education program.

DARE is one of many programs that have been created to educate children and adults about drugs. In 1980 U.S. first lady Nancy Reagan famously launched the "Just Say No to Drugs" campaign. It used media advertisements and school education programs. The catchphrase "Just Say No" is still used in society more than 30 years later. Countless other institutions—from hospitals and universities to private companies and small-town **PTO** groups—run drug-education programs.

One of the key goals in drug education for young people is to discourage them from trying any drugs early, especially the so-called **gateway drugs**, such as cigarettes, alcohol, and marijuana. Gateway drugs are generally easier to obtain than harder drugs, and their effects are not nearly as dangerous as harder drugs. They are also more socially acceptable. For instance, children see adults smoking cigarettes and drinking alcohol on a regular basis. Educators believe that trying these gateway drugs is likely to lead to other drugs. One study showed that children ages 12 to 17 who smoke marijuana are 85 times more likely to use cocaine than those who do not. The belief is that children are far more likely to move on to experimenting with other, more dangerous drugs once they have used gateway drugs.

CASE STUDY

Does Education Work?

Drug educators recognize that, although their programs carry a powerful message, there is no guarantee that the message will stick. Tim Schennum, a California police DARE officer, admitted, "Let's keep in mind that DARE … is still just a forty-five-minute session, once a week, for seventeen weeks. There are many hours when these [children] are exposed to many of life's potential perils."

With more than 30 years of vigorous education against drug use, critics say that these programs have been ineffective. With all this effort, statistics ought to show a dramatic decrease in drug use in teenagers. But this has not happened. A 2002 study by the White House Office of National Drug Control Policy showed the following statistics of illicit drug use among teenagers.

	1985	1996	2001
People ages 12–17 who have ever used illicit drugs	32%	22%	28%
People ages 18–25 who have ever used illicit drugs	63%	48%	55%

A more recent study by the National Institute on Drug Abuse showed these statistics among teenagers:

	2006	2009
8th-graders who have ever used illicit drugs	21%	20%
10th-graders who have ever used illicit drugs	36%	36%
12th-graders who have ever used illicit drugs	48%	47%

Critics of drug education point to statistics like these and judge education efforts as a failure. With the millions of dollars and the countless hours devoted to education, how can nearly half of our teenagers graduate from high school having tried illicit drugs? How could the number of kids who have tried illicit drugs not decrease over a span of several years? The critics ask, where are the statistics proving that drug education is helping to stop kids from using drugs?

FINDING MEANING IN STATISTICS

When reading statistics, it's important to think critically about the data being presented. Here are two ways to think more critically about statistics.

- *Look for missing information.* These statistics show the percentage of people who have ever used illicit drugs *one time*. The statistics do not show how many of those people ever used drugs again. If the statistics showed how many teenagers became **addicted**, the study might be more meaningful.

- *Make your own conclusions.* If 20 percent of eighth-graders have used drugs, then that means 80 percent have never used drugs. Perhaps you think this is actually good news. Some people might have the opinion that without anti-drug education programs, the number of users would actually be much higher.

Educators hope that with more effective education, children and teens will be less likely to try drugs.

Some people who support the legalization of drugs point out a reason why drug education might be failing. From the start, drug educators projected a "zero-tolerance" approach to drugs. The message is: All drugs are dangerous, so don't try any. This was the thrust of the Just Say No campaign: If someone offers you drugs, just say no! In time, this approach was criticized because the attempt to scare people into saying no to all drugs was not realistic. Teenagers see examples in real life that appear to prove, for instance, that using one drug will not necessarily lead to using harder drugs. As they grow up, they may see older siblings or young adults using marijuana, for instance, and see that not all marijuana users become addicted to it. In fact, some lead productive, otherwise normal lives.

Mixed messages

Children and teenagers receive mixed messages in the media about drugs. On the one hand, they see television programs and advertisements that are meant to discourage drug use. But they also see images of people having fun and enjoying doing drugs or drinking alcohol. Some celebrities speak openly about their drug use in a positive way. So young people receive mixed messages: one that shows the danger of drugs, and the other that shows the excitement of drugs.

While some celebrities put forth a consistent, positive image, others become more famous for their repeated, publicized trips to drug or alcohol **rehab**. For more than a half century, celebrities have reached a tragic end through drug abuse. Film stars Judy Garland and Marilyn Monroe both died of accidental prescription drug overdoses, as did the rock stars Elvis Presley, Jimi Hendrix, and Keith Moon of The Who. The 1960s rock singer Janis Joplin died of a heroin overdose. And in 2009 the death of Michael Jackson, one of the greatest pop singers of the century. He had become dependent on a number of prescription drugs and ultimately died from an overdose of a painkiller injected by his personal physicians.

All these celebrities and many others died at relatively young ages, at the peak of their fame. Their deaths did not diminish their fame or glory. In fact, the drug-related deaths may have increased the attention given to them by the media and their fans.

CASE STUDY

Heath Ledger

Heath Ledger was born in 1979 in Perth, Australia. He rose to stardom quickly. After appearing on Australian television as a child actor for several years, he moved to Hollywood and quickly earned roles that brought him to a worldwide audience, such as *10 Things I Hate about You* (1999), *The Patriot* (2000), and *Brokeback Mountain* (2005). Ledger reached the peak of his talents in 2007 by creating the role of the Joker in *The Dark Knight*. But even before the film was seen in theaters, Heath Ledger had died.

Ledger was dedicated to his craft, perhaps too much so. He threw himself into acting roles with such intensity that the roles took over his life, creating anxiety and tension. His relationship with his girlfriend, actress Michelle Williams, was a rocky one and added to his anxiety. He had trouble sleeping and developed chronic insomnia. He was prescribed sleep aids, among other prescription drugs.

On January 22, 2008, Ledger died from an overdose of these legal prescription drugs. He had taken six different kinds of medication including a mix of painkillers, anxiety medication, and a sleep aid. Ledger's father said, "Heath's accidental death serves as a caution to the hidden dangers of combining prescription medications, even at low dosage."

WAVE THE WHITE FLAG?

No matter what evidence you examine, people recognize that drug use is a serious threat to our society. The solution, many believe, is to legalize some or all drugs. The idea may sound strange, but there is a large amount of support for drug legalization.

The Netherlands model

In the Netherlands, the 1970s saw a dramatic explosion in the use of illegal drugs, especially heroin. The Dutch government decided that the best way to address the problems were to target organized crime groups that were running the drug trade while emphasizing treatment of drug abuse to heal their society. In 1976 the Netherlands **decriminalized** the possession of small amounts of all drugs. This meant that it wasn't *legal* to possess heroin, but if you were caught with it, you would be sent to treatment, not jail.

Selling most drugs did remain illegal in the Netherlands. The Dutch identified marijuana and other cannabis drugs (such as hashish) as legal "soft drugs." Almost all other drugs (**cocaine**, heroin, **amphetamines**, etc.) were illegal "hard drugs." And no drugs could be sold to children.

The new laws allowed for cafes to sell a small amount (up to 5 grams) of marijuana. This meant that Dutch cities, such as Amsterdam, became the only places in the world where it was legal for an adult to walk into a business and legally purchase drugs that were banned everywhere else.

What were the results? Among the Dutch population, the use of some drugs appears to have increased slightly. The number of people who smoked marijuana increased by about 3.5 percent. The number of people who used hard drugs increased by smaller margins or not at all.

Critics of drug legalization will point to these statistics as proof that legalizing drugs will lead to an increase in drug use. Critics of drug laws may counter that these statistics do not show the dramatic jump in drug use that others had feared.

Percentage of Dutch population ages 15–64 who have used drugs in their lifetime

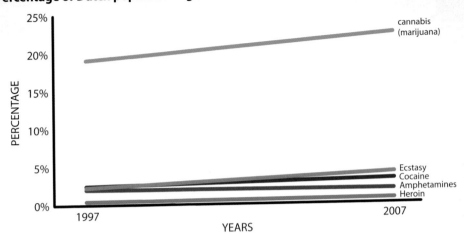

cannabis
(marijuana)

Ecstasy
Cocaine
Amphetamines
Heroin

PERCENTAGE

25%

20%

15%

10%

5%

0%

1997

2007

YEARS

In Amsterdam, people are allowed to buy and use drugs in certain places.

Losing the war on drugs?

Those who argue for legalization of drugs point out that the war on drugs has been a failure. Evidence shows that despite spending billions of dollars to attack the drug supply chain, the war on drugs has had little or no effect on cutting off the flow of drugs. Every year the National Drug Intelligence Center publishes a Threat Assessment document. It explains the availability of every illicit drug in the United States. Here is a sampling of the status of heroin for a decade-long period:

- 2002: "The drug is widely available, and the user population is growing."

- 2004: "Heroin remains readily available throughout most major metropolitan areas."

- 2006: "Heroin is generally available in drug markets throughout the nation."

- 2008: "Heroin is readily available in most large metropolitan areas."

- 2010: "Heroin remains widely available and that availability is increasing in some areas."

Over the course of ten years, the availability of heroin remained strong, despite every effort on the part of the U.S. government to stop the supply chain. These reports provide pretty much the same message about marijuana, **methamphetamine**, and other drugs.

A GOVERNOR FOR LEGALIZATION

Former New Mexico governor Gary E. Johnson recognizes the dire problem with drugs. "For all the money that we're putting into the war on drugs, it is an absolute failure," he says. "By legalizing drugs, we can control them, regulate them, and tax them. If we legalize drugs, we might have a healthier society."

Stop spending to stop the supply

Opponents of drug laws say it's time to give up the battle. Make these drugs legal and stop spending billions of dollars trying to stop them from entering the country. Stop spending billions to arrest, convict, and imprison drug dealers. In 2004, the U.S. government spent $11.7 billion on drug control. Here is how that total is broken down:

$2.9 billion	Treatment (health care for drug users and **addicts**)
$1.4 billion	Prevention (education and other programs to prevent drug use)
$1.2 billion	Research (science and medicine research on drugs)
$3 billion	Law enforcement (police, judges, prisons)
$1.1 billion	International law enforcement (apprehending criminals in other countries)
$2.1 billion	Interdiction (finding and destroying drug crops)

The last three rows—totaling $6.2 billion, or more than 50 percent of the total cost—would be eliminated if drugs were legalized.

Massive spending on the war on drugs affects the economies of countries around the world. In the United Kingdom, a study by the drug-legalization group Transform Drug Policy Foundation estimates that legalizing and regulating drugs would create a total savings of anywhere between $7.3 billion and $22.2 billion. A 2009 estimate stated that Australia spends about $4.7 billion a year to fight the war on drugs.

Lower crime by lowering cost of drugs

One theory in favor of legalizing drugs is that the price of drugs on the street will lower dramatically, and this will benefit society. Because drugs are illegal around the world, transporting drugs into a country is extremely expensive. The drugs must travel a long route of being sold and re-sold before they reach dealers who sell them to users. Each time the drugs are re-sold, the price goes up because the seller needs to make a profit. And because it is an illegal trade, the risks of being caught are high, so everyone involved wants to make a huge profit.

A 2008 study by the Beckley Foundation, a UK nonprofit organization that seeks to change global drug policies, estimated that for cocaine to travel from the farm where coca plants are harvested in South America to a London street where the drug is sold, it would change hands at least five times. Each time, the price would rise dramatically.

So from the farm to the customer, the cost of the cocaine increases by an incredible 993 percent! If cocaine were legal, there would not be such a long and expensive route to market. The sale could be regulated and taxed, and the cost increases would be much more reasonable. The cocaine user who eventually buys the drug would pay much less money.

How is this good for society? Won't this just encourage more people to use cocaine? Yes, some people believe that lower costs might increase use. But the potential benefit is keeping drug addicts out of **poverty** and decreasing the crime associated with drugs. Today, crime rates are high partly because people need to steal to get money to buy drugs. In addition, if drugs such as cocaine and heroin were legalized, violent street gangs and organized crime would no longer be involved in the drug trade. These drugs could possibly be sold in stores like any other regulated products—just as alcohol and tobacco.

Freeing the justice system

People who argue for drug legalization also point out that if drug-related crime is reduced, there will be other benefits to society. Police can focus on preventing other serious crimes if they no longer have to chase down drug makers, dealers, and users.

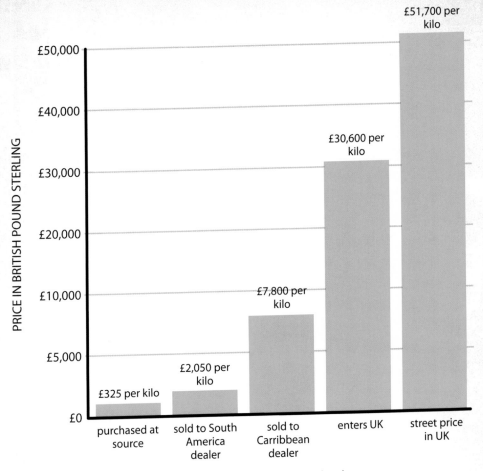

Price Increases for Cocaine Imports

PRICE IN BRITISH POUND STERLING

£51,700 per kilo

£30,600 per kilo

£7,800 per kilo

£2,050 per kilo

£325 per kilo

| purchased at source | sold to South America dealer | sold to Carribbean dealer | enters UK | street price in UK |

■ This graph shows the increase in cost each time cocaine changes hands.

If drug laws were ended, the court system would be unclogged and other, serious criminals would come to trial much sooner. And one of the most pressing issues facing society would be solved: prison overcrowding.

Across the United States, federal, state, and local prisons are bursting at the seams. A 2009 study showed that in 23 states, prisons were over capacity—there were more prisoners living in prisons than these facilities were built to hold. In some prisons, the inmates were sharing beds and did not have adequate medical care. It is an unhealthy and dangerous environment.

In some prisons, overcrowding is a major issue. Prisoners live in very cramped quarters, which leads to crime and the spread of disease. Some people say that ending drug laws can instantly solve the prison-overcrowding problem.

In 2004, there were about 1.3 million people in state prisons in the United States, and 20 percent of them were imprisoned for a drug crime of some kind. If drugs were made legal, some argue that many of these prisoners could be set free and instantly help solve the prison overcrowding problem.

People who make this argument do not propose setting violent criminals free. Most of the drug-crime prisoners did not commit violent crimes. They were convicted of possession or trafficking drugs. A report by The Sentencing Project states that "in 87% of [drug] cases no weapon was involved." Other options include parole and probation, which are also a lot cheaper than sending someone to prison.

LET DRUG USERS GET TREATMENT, NOT PRISON

Another key argument in favor of drug legalization concerns the treatment of drug users in society. Clearly there will always be people who want to try drugs, and no matter what laws are in place, they will find a way to use drugs. By legalizing drugs, these people will no longer be seen as criminals, but rather as humans who have a problem or an illness. And in a humane society, we help people who have illnesses. We do not treat people who are addicted to cigarettes as criminals despite the harm they do to themselves. We do not treat people who drink alcohol as criminals—unless they cross the line and harm others through inappropriate drunken behavior, such as fighting or driving while drunk.

ALCOHOL PROHIBITION

Those who favor drug legalization point out that less than a century ago, another set of laws banned substances that many people wanted to use, and that effort ended in failure. Back in the 1920s, the United States banned alcohol, and many critics of today's drug laws point to the Prohibition era (explained below) as a model of failure. They say that our present multinational drug **prohibition** suffers from many of Prohibition's flaws.

In the early 1800s, the Temperance movement arose in many countries. Influenced by religious teachings, Temperance activists, many of whom were women, pushed for governments to ban the use of alcohol because they thought it was an evil temptation. They believed alcohol led directly to violent crimes. They believed that men should stop wasting their earnings on alcohol and support their families instead.

In some countries, local governments responded by passing local bans on alcohol. For instance, Canadian provinces began banning alcohol in 1900 and continued for the next 20 years, but a nationwide ban was never passed. In 1916, the government of Ontario, Canada, passed laws that banned the *consumption* of alcohol but allowed alcohol to be produced. So companies made alcohol and exported it—selling it out of the province, mostly to the United States.

In the United States, individual states were also passing laws that banned alcohol through the 1910s. But the country went a giant step further than Canada. In 1920, the U.S. Congress passed the Eighteenth Amendment to the Constitution, banning the **manufacture**, sale, and transportation of alcohol. By the date of its passage, 33 states had already banned alcohol. The amendment launched the era of Prohibition in America, which would last for 13 years.

Despite the act of Congress, alcohol did not disappear, nor did American adults' thirst for it. Although beer consumption declined (because beer was difficult to make and store illegally), the use of wine and hard liquors such as gin actually increased during Prohibition, even though they were illegal. People set up small family businesses by traveling to Canada to purchase alcohol and illegally transport it back to the United States to sell. Other people went to work as "bootleggers," people who made and distributed illegal alcohol on their own. Much of the liquor was sold in illegal bars called speakeasies.

This photo from the Prohibition era shows illegal beer being poured into the sewers so that nobody could drink it.

Many of the bootlegging operations and speakeasies were controlled by gangsters. These organized gangs of criminals bribed police officials and forcefully took over individuals' alcohol businesses. Perhaps the most famous gangster was Al Capone of Chicago. Organized crime gangs engaged in violent fights with each other for control of neighborhoods in cities. They also fought with the local police and federal agents who attempted to stop their illegal activities. With machine guns blazing, gangsters brought terror and fear to American streets.

Crime rates skyrocketed during Prohibition. In just the first year, the U.S. crime rate increased 24 percent. In the 13 years of Prohibition, the number of prisoners in federal prisons increased by 561 percent. More than two-thirds of those in prison had been arrested on alcohol and drug charges.

Law enforcement agents made these arrests and were sometimes successful in breaking up bootlegging operations and closing down speakeasies. Many photographs from the era show barrels of alcohol being poured down sewer drains to prevent it from being distributed. But for the most part, the government proved unable to stop the flow of alcohol during Prohibition.

When the Great Depression hit the United States in 1929, Prohibition was doomed. With the national economy in crisis, new businesses and jobs were needed. The country needed the alcohol industry to be made legal to help the economy. In addition, Americans recognized that Prohibition was not working: Americans still drank alcohol, and society was in a terrible state with the rise of organized crime. Eventually, Congress passed the Twenty-first Amendment, ending Prohibition in 1933. Some states, however, continued their local prohibitions against alcohol for many years after that. Today, some states and counties ban alcohol sales on Sundays, and certain towns and counties have various forms of alcohol prohibition.

■ Bootlegging was one of the major criminal activities involving the notorious gangster, Al Capone.

Comparing alcohol Prohibition to today's drug laws

You can use graphic organizers to help organize your thoughts on a topic. Here's a helpful way of comparing Prohibition with today's drug situation. You can copy the following graphic organizer onto a piece of paper and fill in the rest of the spaces. Complete each sentence by marking an X under the phrase that you think makes sense.

	the same as during Prohibition	similar to Prohibition	very different from Prohibition
The increase or decrease in the number of drug users is …			
The crime rate is …			
Government's ability to stop sales of illegal substances is …			
Power of organized crime is …			
Changes in prison population is …			

DRAWING CONCLUSIONS

- Does the comparison between Prohibition and today's drug situation help you form an opinion about whether drugs should be legalized?
- If so, what is your opinion?

THE MOVE TO MAKE MARIJUANA LEGAL

While it may be hard to imagine all illicit drugs being legalized, marijuana legalization may be just around the corner. In recent years, many countries have relaxed their marijuana laws or the penalties for marijuana convictions. Some countries treat marijuana offenses as civil offenses (like a speeding ticket) rather than as a criminal offense (punishable by large fines and prison time). Countries such as Australia, Mexico, Portugal, and the Netherlands have all relaxed their marijuana laws.

Medical marijuana

The use of **medical marijuana** is providing a boost to marijuana-legalization advocates. Smoking marijuana is an effective painkiller for symptoms of several illnesses, including cancer, AIDS, and multiple sclerosis. For instance, chemotherapy treatment for cancer can cause nausea and vomiting, which marijuana relieves. AIDS patients tend to lack appetite, and smoking marijuana increases appetite. And the pain caused by diseases such as arthritis, Crohn's disease, and migraines is alleviated by marijuana.

Opponents of medical marijuana say that symptoms should be treated with other drugs, but some patients report that marijuana is the only treatment that helps them. A California woman named Angel Raich, who suffers from wasting disease, has found that marijuana is the only drug that helps relieve her symptoms. She said, "Without cannabis, my life would be a death sentence."

In 1996, California became the first U.S. state to make it legal to grow, possess, sell, and use marijuana for medical purposes. A patient must have a recommendation from a doctor to be able to purchase the substance. Suddenly, a legal industry of growing and selling marijuana sprang up in California. Stores were opened where marijuana was sold, and people flocked to California from other states to purchase the medication. Other states followed suit. From Alaska to Maine, more than a dozen states passed laws legalizing medical marijuana.

Why not ban alcohol?

Even hard-line advocates for drug laws recognize that marijuana use creates milder effects and fewer health risks than other drugs. Critics of drug laws often compare marijuana to alcohol and point out that alcohol is probably the more dangerous substance. Tim Hollis, one of the top police chiefs in the United Kingdom, said in 2010, "My personal belief is that in terms of sheer scale of harm, one of the most dangerous drugs in this country is alcohol."

	Alcohol	Marijuana
Addiction	Alcohol is addictive.	Experts disagree on whether marijuana is addictive.
Long-Term Health Risks	Alcohol contributes to heart disease, liver disease, and several forms of cancer, among other serious illnesses.	Scientific studies have not proven that marijuana causes death or disease.
Motor Skills	Alcohol seriously harms motor skills, making it dangerous to drive a car. Alcohol leads to approximately 30 percent of all U.S. traffic deaths.	Marijuana harms motor skills. It is not safe to drive a car after using marijuana.
Overdose	It is possible to drink so much that you will die.	It is virtually impossible to die of a marijuana overdose.

When comparing the two substances, most people decide that alcohol is, in fact, the more dangerous, and they wonder why it is legal while marijuana is banned. It is also important to point out that like any substance, marijuana use can have negative consequences. Many people turn this around and conclude: They're both dangerous substances, so both should be banned.

INDIVIDUAL LIBERTIES

One other argument is used by those who want to legalize drugs. The argument is one of individual rights. The key to **democracy** is that adult citizens have the rights to "life, liberty, and the pursuit of happiness." These rights are not given to us by our government; these rights are "natural"—they simply exist and cannot be changed.

Some people say that part of these natural rights is the right to treat our bodies in any way we please. If we wish to eat only vegetables and no meats, that is our right. If we wish to train our bodies to be athletes, that is our right. These choices may seem like healthy ones. But whether the choice is good doesn't really matter. What does matter is that you have the right to choose. What you do with the right is up to you. Yes, you do have the right to make stupid choices, just as long as your stupidity does not trample anyone else's life, liberty, or pursuit of happiness. We will soon look at the other side of this argument.

So, according to anti-drug law arguments, an adult has the right to smoke cigarettes even though science has proven this may cause cancer. An adult has the right to drink alcohol, even though alcohol abuse could lead to addiction and even death. The basic idea is that adult citizens have the right to put any substance into their bodies, and the government should not have the power to decide that one substance is allowed, while a different substance is not.

RIGHT OR WRONG?

Do you think it would be right or wrong to allow each adult citizen to decide whether to use drugs or not?

Lazy citizens

A further argument along these lines is that when governments make decisions for us, we become lazy citizens. We come to rely on governments deciding what's best for us, and we abandon our responsibility to make intelligent decisions about our own lives. Read the following interview with a teenager in Britain who was arrested for possession of the synthetic drug mephedrone.

"Me and my mate [friend] decided to buy this drug. We bought 20 grams off the Internet for £200 … it was quite easy. It just came in the post [mail]. I decided to go to my mate's house party. I did quite a lot of this drug and [freaked out]. They arrested me, and the nurse at the police station said I've got to go [to] hospital because I was dying. I was sweating loads … my [pulse] was 200…. I woke up two days later with all these tubes hanging out of me. Obviously, I think, you know if you can get it off the Internet, it can't be that bad…. The police … arrested me for having the drug. They tested in the lab and … it came back as mephedrone. I thought it was a legal drug … so I'm getting punished for buying a legal drug, but it's coming back as illegal. I think these websites should be shut down."

Think about what this teenager is saying. Do you think he is taking responsibility for his actions? Or do you think he's blaming others for his nearly killing himself with mephedrone? Critics of drug laws contend that in a society where so many things are illegal, people are losing the ability to take responsibility. Like this teenager, people assume, "Well, if you can buy it in a store, it's got to be safe." Or, "If this were too dangerous to use, then it would be illegal." People grow up trained to think that someone will always save them from making bad decisions.

■ Adults have the right to choose the legal ways in which they treat their bodies. Those who are good citizens make responsible choices.

The effect on society

According to advocates for drug laws, drug use affects a much wider circle of people than just friends or relatives. Think about the effects on all of us—on the community or society—that occur every time drugs cause someone to need emergency medical attention or to lose a job or to create a public disturbance. Society is affected because of the cost of medical treatment. Society is affected because a jobless person goes on welfare. Society is affected because the police who come to that public disturbance could be elsewhere protecting other people.

PROTECTING OTHERS

There are many arguments against the idea that drugs should be legalized to allow people to exercise their rights. Some say that it's wrong to think that individual rights allow a person to do anything—because many times our actions affect other people.

Using drugs can cause damage to much more than the person who is using. Consider:

- Slaven Relja was a journalist in the European country of Croatia who at age thirty-three started using heroin. He developed an addiction that destroyed his ability to work. He made up news stories that he wrote. He had to spend so much money on his drug addiction that he stole money from people he worked with and even sold his family's silverware. His life fell apart, and he wound up in a rehabilitation community, where after much hard work he did recover.

- In July 2009, twenty-one-year-old Gregory Dionisio got behind the wheel of his car after he had been drinking—and also having used marijuana, cocaine, and ecstasy. Driving down a Connecticut road in the early morning, Dionisio drove his car on the wrong side of the road and crashed into a man named Thomas Fleming, who was riding his motorcycle. A husband and father, Fleming died soon after the crash.

In these scenarios, does one person's drug use affect just that person? Or has one person's drug use affected others, too? Who is protecting the rights of the people who were affected by these drug users' actions? This is why people believe governments should control drug use—because there is no way to contain the damaging effects of drugs.

Each person takes on responsibilities as a citizen. Yes, we have individual rights, but we also have the responsibility of respecting the rights of everyone else in society. Some people believe each person should be able to make those decisions without the interference of government. Others believe government is needed to ensure that each person's rights are preserved. What do you think?

■ People make choices, both good and bad, every day. Each choice brings consequences. When next confronted with a difficult situation, what choice will you make?

YOU DECIDE: WHO IS THE VICTIM?

One argument in favor of ending drug laws is that using drugs is a personal choice, and that people's choices affect only themselves. If there is a victim of drug use, then it is the user and nobody else. So why should the government spend billions of dollars to carry out laws that stop people from harming themselves?

Sometimes it's difficult to decide who the victim is in different situations. Sometimes, a person will do something wrong, but that action clearly affects only themselves. There is no other victim. Other times, a person's actions can affect other people in a lot of unpredictable ways. In these cases, there may be other victims.

Read the following scenarios and think about the questions that follow each scenario.

Ethan is sixteen years old. He buys 1 gram of marijuana from a dealer on a playground. One night, he smokes it by himself when his parents are not home. He spends the night watching TV and then goes to bed. He decides that marijuana didn't do much for him, and he never uses it again.

- Who is the victim?
- Does Ethan's story help you decide whether or not recreational use of marijuana be illegal?

Chakira is twenty-one years old. She drinks four beers at a party and then drives herself home. Although she arrives home safely, her blood-alcohol level is above the legal limit while she is driving.

- Who is the victim?
- Should alcohol be banned for all adult users?

Felix is twenty-five years old. He goes to an all-ages concert at a downtown music club. At the concert, Felix mingles in the crowd and sells ecstasy to people he meets. Some of his customers are under eighteen.

- Who is the victim?
- Should it be a crime to sell drugs to underage users?

Lauren is a thirty-year-old woman whose husband, Dave, received a medical marijuana prescription to help him cope with his chronic back pain. They live in a state where medical marijuana is legal. Frequently Dave tells Lauren that he doesn't need all of the marijuana on his prescription to ease his pain, so he has leftovers. He invites her to use the marijuana if she wants.

- Who is the victim?
- Should it be a crime to use medical marijuana for non-medical purposes?

Ashley is 17 years old and has been smoking marijuana with her friends for about a year. Ashley shares a bedroom with her 14-year-old sister, Eliza. Ashley doesn't realize it, but Eliza knows about Ashley's drug use. Eliza accidentally finds a few of Ashley's marijuana cigarettes in their room and decides to take them. The following weekend, Eliza smokes the marijuana with her friends at a sleepover.

- Who is the victim?
- Do you think Eliza would have started using drugs if Ashley had not been a drug user?

Diego is a 20-year-old college student. He has been using cocaine for several months and starts using it more and more often. In just one semester he spends more than $3,000 on the drug. He flunks out of college, and his parents cannot get a refund of the $22,000 they paid for his tuition. His parents place him in a rehab program that costs $15,000 for one month of treatment.

- Who is the victim?
- Should Diego's parents make him pay back the money they lost on his drug use?

GLOSSARY

addict person who has developed a drug-use habit that he or she cannot break

addicted unable to stop using a drug

amphetamines drug used medically to increase the activity of the central nervous system

cannabinoid chemical made from THC, the chemical found in the hemp plant that reacts in the human body to make people "high"

cannabis any of the drugs, such as marijuana and hashish, that are made from the hemp plant

cocaine drug made from coca leaves that is most often sniffed as a powder

decriminalized removed penalties from an act that would send people to prison

democracy a government in which the supreme power is held by the people

drug lord person who heads a large criminal organization that produces and transports illegal drugs

ecstasy drug, also called MDMA, that makes some users have feelings of tremendous emotions of joy or love

gateway drug substance that is relatively easy to get and has milder effects than other drugs; this substance is called a "gateway" drug because many people start using it before moving on to more dangerous drugs

hallucination fake vision that people see after they have taken certain drugs

hashish drug prepared from the flowering tops of the hemp plant. It is smoked, chewed, or drunk.

heroin drug made from poppy plants that is smoked or injected into the body in liquid form

high feeling a drug user gets after taking certain drugs

illicit illegal; forbidden by law

legal high substance that is sold legally but has effects on the user that are similar to illegal drugs

LSD illegal drug that causes abnormal sensations, exagerated emotions, time and space confusion, and hallucinations

manufacture to make a product

marijuana dried leaves from the hemp plant that are smoked like a cigarette

MDMA abbreviation for the drug Methylenedioxymethamphetamine, also known as ecstasy

medical marijuana marijuana that is used by patients to ease the pain of symptoms of diseases

mephedrone synthetic drug similar to ecstasy

metabolism the processes by which a substance is handled in the body

methamphetamine drug created from amphetamine that is used illegally as a stimulant of the central nervous system

organized crime large groups of people formed into an organization to do illegal activities together

performance-enhancing drugs (PED) drugs taken by athletes to increase muscle mass, strength, vision or other athletic abilities

poverty lack of money or possessions

prohibition banning of a product or an act; from the word prohibit, which means to stop or restrict

psychosis mental disorder in which a person cannot tell real from unreal

PTO abbreviation for Parent Teacher Organization. A formal organization that consists of parents, teachers and school staff. Its purpose is to encourage volunteerism and community building within the school.

rehab abbreviation for rehabilitation. To restore to a condition of health or functional activity

synthetic made in a factory or in a lab; not grown naturally

terrorist person who uses terror to achieve a certain goal

testosterone hormone produced in the human body that helps create male sex organs and other male physical features, such as muscle mass and body hair

tobacco leafy plant used to make cigarettes

trafficker person carrying illegal substances from one country into another

treatment medical care or counseling to solve a health or mental issue

FURTHER INFORMATION

Books

Balkin, Karen F. Club *Drugs*. Detroit: Greenhaven Press, 2005.

Barbour, Scott. *Should Marijuana Be Legalized?* San Diego, CA: ReferencePoint Press, 2010.

Bjornlund, Lydia D. *How Dangerous Are Performance-Enhancing Drugs?* San Diego, CA: ReferencePoint Press, 2011.

Dudley, William (ed.). *Drugs and Sports.* San Diego, CA: Greenhaven Press, 2001

Gallas, Judith C. *Drugs and Sports.* San Diego: Lucent Books, 1997.

Gottfried, Ted. *Marijuana.* New York: Marshall Cavendish Benchmark, 2010.

Gottfried, Ted. *Should Drugs Be Legalized?* Brookfield, CT: Twenty-First Century Books, 2000.

LeVert, Suzanne. *Ecstasy.* New York: Marshall Cavendish Benchmark, 2010.

Marcovitz, Hal. *Drug & Alcohol Abuse.* Broomall, PA: Mason Crest, 2007

Masline, Shelagh Ryan. *Drug Abuse and Teens: A Hot Issue.* Berkeley Heights, NJ: Enslow Publishers, 2000.

Menhard, Francha Roffe. *Inhalents.* New York: Marshall Cavendish Benchmark, 2010.

Mezinski, Pierre, Melissa Daly & Francoise Jaud. *Drugs Explained: The Real Deal on Alcohol, Pot, Ecstasy, and More.* New York: Amulet Books, 2004.

Palenque, Stephanie Maher. *Crack & Cocaine = Busted!*. Berkeley Heights, NJ: Enslow Publishers, 2005.

Websites

www.checkyourself.com
A website where teens, athletes, and celebrities post descriptions of their "moments of truth"—the times when they realized they had drug problems and decided to solve them.

www.dare.com
Website for the worldwide drug-education organization.

www.leap.cc
Website for an organization of law enforcement officers (Law Enforcement Against Prohibition (LEAP)) who believe that it would be more effective to regulate drugs rather than prohibit them.

www.nida.nih.gov/JSP4/JSP.html
Website with resources for teenagers run by the National Institute of Health, a federal government agency.

www.drugfreeworld.org
Watch videos and learn more about drug-education programs.

INDEX